BRITISH MEMORIALS
OF THE
GREAT WAR
1914-1918.

The Naval & Military Press Ltd

Published by

The Naval & Military Press Ltd
Unit 5 Riverside, Brambleside
Bellbrook Industrial Estate
Uckfield, East Sussex
TN22 1QQ England

Tel: +44 (0)1825 749494

www.naval-military-press.com
www.nmarchive.com

In reprinting in facsimile from the original, any imperfections are inevitably reproduced and the quality may fall short of modern type and cartographic standards.

ZEEBRUGGE

Description of this memorial on page 14.

[Photo: *Central Press.*

PREFACE

This book has been specially prepared for the purpose of supplying information about the British memorials erected in Belgium and France to those who fell in the Great War. A few details are given of the Memorials to the Missing and National Memorials, and the order followed is from Zeebrugge towards Switzerland. Next in order are the Divisional Memorials followed by those to Regiments, Battalions, Brigades, etc. ; finally, to this has been added a list of memorials in other parts of the world which has been strictly confined to those erected by the Imperial War Graves Commission. The lists are preceded by a brief account of the most momentous episodes of the war on the Western Front.

In a few pages, only the baldest outline is possible, and as such it is offered as an aid to those who intend visiting these scenes of devastation and fortitude, which for generations will draw men and women from the ends of the earth. The psychological and educational value of a few hours spent round Ypres and the Somme can only be understood by those who have had the experience ; on the battlefields, recent history lives, and memorials like Menin Gate, Tyne Cot and Thiepval speak more directly and poignantly than any book, drama or picture.

It is not perhaps generally known that British soldiers lie in 15,705 Burial grounds scattered throughout 108 different countries and islands, and that of 1,285,751 dead, the graves of 517,771 are unknown.

The assistance of the Imperial War Graves Commission, given always most cordially and willingly, has made easier the collecting of scattered data, and our thanks are due for the material supplied and the courtesy shown ; it is only correct to add that the Commission is in no way responsible for any statement made.

Many books, pamphlets and individuals with personal knowledge have been consulted in writing the short account of the war, and the outline of battles given in Everyman's Encyclopaedia was of special value.

Practically every British memorial in Belgium and France will be found on the maps enclosed in the cover ; these four maps of the principal war areas were prepared by Dean & Dawson, Ltd. mainly from information supplied by the Imperial War Graves Commission.

The distance from important centres, where there are excellent facilities for visiting memorials, is given in kilometres, which is the unit of measurement in Belgium and France ; conversion is simple when one remembers that 8 kilometres are 5 miles.

DEAN & DAWSON LTD.

MENIN GATE, Ypres.

Description of this memorial on page 16.

[Photo: *Central Press.*

The Western Front 1914—1918.

1914

The ultimate causes of the War were human and therefore inscrutable ; despite the assiduous study of Psychology, we are still unable to give an adequate explanation or analysis of the commonest emotion ; the Sarajevo murders have in consequence been arbitrarily selected as the beginning of this bald outline of the principal battles in which the British Armies were engaged on the Western Front. On June 28th, 1914, a Bosnian student named Prinzip shot the Austrian Archduke Francis Ferdinand (nephew and heir of the Emperor Francis Joseph) and his wife at Sarajevo and both died shortly afterwards. This involved a dispute between Austria and Serbia ; Russia supporting the latter and Germany the former ; France, Belgium and Great Britain were drawn into the diplomatic correspondence and in the end a state of war existed with Russia, Serbia, France, Belgium and Great Britain arrayed against Germany, Austria and Hungary ; the war may be said to have begun on August 4th when diplomatic relations were severed between Great Britain and Germany.

On August 7th, the Germans entered Liège and within a week a great part of her army swept over a large section of Belgium ; part of the Belgian Army retreated towards Antwerp and on August 26th, Germany had her first noted success when the forts of Namur fell. As only a skeleton of the Central Powers' forces faced Russia, Germany was free to concentrate her armies on the Allied armies of France, Belgium and Great Britain in Flanders and France, which was known throughout the War as the " Western Front."

During August, 1914, over 100,000 British soldiers known as the British Expeditionary Force (B.E.F.) and also later as the " Old Contemptibles " under the command of Sir John French, crossed the Channel, 70,000 of whom took up a position on the left of the 5th French army near Mons.

On August 23rd the B.E.F. first came into contact with the German army. but as the German forces were far superior in numbers and equipment, the B.E.F. was ultimately compelled to retreat as far as le Cateau where on August 26th they made a stand against the Germans, inflicting on them severe losses. A further retreat was necessary and the Marne was reached on September 3rd where it was decided to resist the invading forces ; the battle lasted from September 6th to

September 12th and on the following day the Germans were forced back across the Aisne. It is generally admitted that this Battle of the Marne had a determining influence on the whole history of the War ; after the Marne defeat the Germans tried to reach the coast and failed.

The Belgian forces having retreated at the beginning on Antwerp, were reinforced by the British Naval and Royal Marine Brigades and tried to hold the city, but on October 9th Antwerp fell.

The Germans in their effort to reach the coast were frustrated by the action of the Belgians who opened the sluices of the Yser canal at Nieuport, flooding the country as far as Dixmude ; before the middle of October an attack was made by the Germans on Ypres and the climax of the battle was reached on October 31st when the German attempt to break through at Gheluvelt failed ; more than twelve divisions of the Germans, amongst whom were the Prussian Guard, made a fierce onslaught on the British forces on November 11th, driving back the first division, but counter-attacks recovered most of the lost positions. Ypres was destined to be the centre of most desperate fighting, not only in 1914 but also in 1915, 1916, 1917 and 1918 ; in and around Ypres during the War about 250,000 of our men lost their lives, which was nearly one-fourth of the total British soldiers killed. After the resistance of 1914, Ypres became a test of fortitude and endurance and the determination to hold it at all costs inspired the soldiers at the front and the Government and people at home. Verdun in 1916 had a similar significance for the French and the effect of the fall of either might have had very serious consequences ; the cost in human lives both at Ypres and Verdun was appalling.

At the end of 1914 the mining and industrial resources of Belgium were under the control of Germany, as well as some of the coalfields of Northern France. Great Britain was obliged to train and equip masses of troops which had volunteered from every part of the Empire. After 1914, open warfare was replaced by trench fighting.

1915

During the winter of 1914-15, fighting practically ceased and preparations were made for a Spring offensive. The British attacked on March 10th at Neuve Chapelle where the Indian Corps displayed great courage and resistance, though the casualties were very heavy ; the French made their attack at Woevre ; the losses on both sides were staggering.

On April 22nd a counter-offensive was made by the Germans against Ypres, in which they used phosgene and chlorine gasses ; the resistance to this new method of warfare revealed the mettle and indomitable character of the Canadian troops ; this gas attack north-east of Ypres coincided with an attack on Hill 60 where the fighting was of the fiercest character ; the battle for Hill 60 lasted for five days and at the end of this period the British troops still held what remained of the Hill. These struggles around Ypres are known as the second battle of Ypres and lasted from April 22nd until May 25th. After this the German attack slackened here in order to meet the Allied attacks in front of Lens where there were massive fortifications ; on September 23rd, an intense bombardment on a wide front was opened by the Allies extending from La Bassèe to Arras, and in Champagne ; the battle of Loos was the principal British effort ; the advance on September 25th after the bombardment was successful ; the Hohenzollern Redoubt was taken and Hulluch reached. The 15th Division took the village of Loos and Hill 70, although later the British Forces were driven back. The casualties in the battle of Loos were about 50,000. Some progress was made on the slopes of Vimy Ridge which dominated the whole neighbourhood.

German successes in the near East forced the attention of the British Government on Gallipoli, where a landing was effected at the end of April. This landing forms one of the most thrilling episodes of the War, where the Australian and New Zealand Forces distinguished themselves by scaling a series of steep cliffs and with the most dogged determination succeeded in obtaining a foothold ; the losses were terrible, but the courage displayed by the troops will live long in the annals of the War. It was obvious now that the War would be one of slow attrition ; the year 1915 was a dark one for the British whose casualties were over 280,000.

1916

At the beginning of 1916, although Germany had failed to obtain her objective in Flanders she had had great success Eastwards during the previous year. Constantinople, the Baghdad Railway and the Balkans were mainly under her direction. She was producing munitions in vast quantities and providing substitutes for materials which she could not import. She planned attacks at Verdun early in 1916 which were to be followed by an attack on the whole Western Front, it being her aim to forestall the Allied attack on the Somme ; Germany opened her offensive against the French at Verdun in February and the attack continued with little interruption till the end of June when the campaign on the Somme began. Verdun was a great victory for the French and very costly to the Germans.

At the end of 1915 Sir Douglas Haig had taken over the command and the battle of the Somme began on July 1st, with its terrible list of casualties.

During the winter of 1915-16 the Germans had constructed in the Bapaume Ridge vast underground chambers ; villages had been transformed into fortresses which no artillery could destroy, and some of these were found intact after the advance of the British troops ; in this fight the troops from Newfoundland revealed their value but their losses were proportionately high.

Before the end of July the Germans were driven out of Longueval and Delville Wood where the South Africans fought with great tenacity and won lasting renown ; on July 23rd the Australians stormed Pozières and the Allies had broken through the first and second defensive systems of the Germans.

On August 18th a general advance was made from Guillemont to Thiepval and about a month later an allied attack took place on a six mile front from Ginchy to Courcelette. On September 15th during this advance heavily-armoured cars on caterpillar wheels were first used ; they were known during the War as Tanks. They gave great assistance to the infantry and had all the advantage of a surprise. The final advance of the year was on November 11th at the battle of the Ancre and progress continued for a week until bad weather brought the movement to a close. In casualties the Somme offensive cost the Allies probably as much as the Germans had suffered at Verdun.

The end of 1916 witnessed a little more optimism amongst the Allies than the previous year. It had now become a question of reserves and the Germans were beginning to consider peace proposals ; the losses that she had sustained during 1916 in the West, the success in her programme of " Drang nach Osten " and the uncertainty of the future, led her to consider peace.

1917

Throughout 1916 the United States Government was at one time irritated by the British blockade, at another greatly enraged with the German submarine campaign. In addition, it was the year of the Presidential election, and consequently no decisive step was taken. When the election was over, the situation was viewed in a freer atmosphere. On April 2nd the President asked for a declaration of war on Germany. On June 25th the first contingent of American troops landed in France.

During the early part of 1917 the Allies forced the Germans to retreat to the heavily-fortified and well-prepared Hindenburg lines ; in this retreat the Germans defended key-positions tenaciously, whilst they evacuated whole villages without a struggle. On March 13th Germany abandoned her strong position on the Bapaume Ridge and four days later Bapaume fell.

The Battle of Arras began on April 9th and on the 12th Vimy Ridge was "taken by storm." In this battle the Ridge was brilliantly attacked by the Canadians. A French Minister said : " Canada won Vimy Ridge and it belongs to her." South of the Hindenburg Line on April 16th an attack was launched along the Aisne heights by the French ; this was called the " second battle of the Aisne " and lasted more than a month ; it ultimately failed.

A serious attack was made by the British in Flanders, at the battle of Messines, the signal for which was the explosion of nineteen mines, and this battle lasted from the 7th to the 12th of June, and succeeded in consolidating the Messines-Wytschaete Ridge.

The third battle of Ypres, which was also known as the Battle of Flanders, lasted from the end of July until the beginning of November ; particularly heavy attacks on the Menin Road were repulsed on September 22nd. Abnormally bad weather hindered progress during the whole of the summer ; St. Julien and Pilekem were taken, and Langemarck captured after an attack which was begun on August 9th.

Before the end of September, Polygon Wood and Zonnebeke were taken and on October 4th the British line ran from Reutel along the ridge to Poelcapelle. On November 10th a successful assault was made on the main ridge at Passchendaele by the Canadians and other British troops. This battle was fought in face of almost insurmountable difficulties and was overcome by the splendid heroism of the troops.

Ludendorff writes a description of Passchendaele in July 1917 from the view-point of the defenders : " The horror of the shell-hole area of Verdun was surpassed. It was no longer life at all. It was mere unspeakable suffering. And through this world of mud the attackers (the British) dragged themselves, slowly but steadily, and in dense masses. Caught in the advance zone by our hail of fire they often collapsed, and the lonely man in the shell-hole breathed again. Then the mass came on again."

From November 20th to the 23rd the British made considerable gains at Cambrai, where instead of initial bombardment, tanks were used, but the cost in lives to Britain was considerable.

Italy had not been successful during 1917, France had practically reached the limit of her man power, and Britain was fast approaching that stage. The Russian revolution had eased the situation for Germany—on the other hand America was hastily preparing for 1918. During the month of November an Allied conference was held in an attempt to introduce unity at the various important fronts, and in December an Allied Naval Council was set up to co-ordinate naval policy.

1918

At a secret session of the Reichstag held in February, it was revealed that the military leaders had determined on a supreme effort before the American troops could arrive in great numbers. It was estimated that the losses to the German army would amount to about one and a half millions. The essence of the plan was surprise and swiftness. As early as November 1917 Ludendorff had decided that " the British must be beaten," and the second battle of the Somme began at dawn on March 21st, mainly against the British Fifth Army, which was composed of 14 divisions. They were opposed by about 40 German divisions, and 20 more divisions attacked the Third British Army. Both the Third and Fifth British Armies were forced to yield, and on March 26th Bapaume was evacuated. The attack on the British, north of the Somme, synchronised with an offensive against the French south of the Somme ; the idea being to separate the two armies and drive a wedge towards Amiens between them. At this juncture Marshal Foch was appointed Commander-in-Chief of the Allied Armies, and on April 4th the Germans were brought to a standstill on the line Oise-Arras. On April 9th at Lys another effort was made by the Germans, their objective being Armentièrs on the Ypres section as a stepping-stone to the Channel Ports ; this offensive was on a vast scale, and Mount Kemmel was gained after terrible fighting which continued until the end of the month ; all attempts, however, to pierce the Ypres defences failed. At Givenchy and Festubert the Germans suffered severe reverses, 750 prisoners and 70 machine guns being taken by one division which was opposed by the highly trained Fourth Ersatz Division and not a yard of the British position was lost. As a set off against this, the Germans had taken the Messines-Wytschaete Ridge and the outskirts of Armentières and Merville. At this time Lord Haig issued his famous order which ended with the words " Each one of us must fight to the end."

On April 30th all movement came to a standstill, but in March and April the British Army had 303,000 casualties. The report of the arrival of the American troops during this period had a great effect on the morale of the troops, and on July 2nd the President of the United States was able to announce that over one million men had sailed.

In May the Germans launched an attack on the Chemin des Dames in addition to one between Rheims and Soissons. So serious were these attacks and so successful from the Germans' point of view that in a short time the French lost all that they had gained since 1914, and were back on the Aisne. The men taken prisoners at this time alone were about 50,000, but in the words of von Kuhl " the Germans had gone fatally too far." The British troops who had been sent to the assistance of the French had been weakened after the fierce fighting in March and April, and were unable to hold the line. The Germans took Soissons on May 29th and next day they had reached the Marne between Chateau-Thierry and Dormans. The French army was reinforced by divisions of young American soldiers who were to prove their mettle at Chateau-Thierry and other points.

The last German offensive was made in the neighbourhood of Rheims in the middle of July ; they advanced three miles across the Marne but their advance was soon afterwards turned into a retreat.

At the end of June the German army was estimated to comprise 207 divisions—more than a half of whom were in the lines. On July 18th the Allied forces were counter-attacking practically all along the line, and soon the turning point of the war was reached. On July 19th the Germans had recrossed the Marne, and before the attacks of the French and American troops they were falling back on the Vesle and on the Aisne. Shortly after the retreat of the Germans, Marshal Foch planned three simultaneous attacks ; one in Flanders, another on the Hindenburg Line and the third in the Argonne.

The principal battles fought by the British armies in the course of these operations achieved the following results :—**The Battle of Amiens August 8th-12th**—freed the railway between Amiens and Paris. **The Battle of Bapaume August 21st-31st**—obliged the Germans to retreat to the east bank of the Somme. **The Battle of Arras August 26th-September 3rd**—forced the Germans back on the outer defences of the Hindenburg Line. The direct result of these three battles was the evacuation by the Germans of Lens, Merville, Bailleul and Mount Kemmel. **The Battle of Epéhy September 18th-19th**—broke through the outer Hindenburg defences. **The Battle of Cambrai—St. Quentin September 27th-October 10th** is considered by some to be the greatest victory of all. The German prisoners taken in this battle were more numerous than in any other engagement in the war. The Canal du Nord was stormed by the victorious forces and they advanced to Cambrai and the last of the defences in the rear of the Hindenburg Line. Before the close of the first battle of Cambrai, the British Second Army and the Belgian Army were forcing the enemy back from Ypres. The second Battle of Cambrai forced the evacuation by the Germans of Cambrai and St. Quentin. **The Battle of Courtrai October 14th-31st** —forced the Germans to abandon the Belgian coast. With this battle the road between Ypres and Menin was freed—the road which had halted British soldiers for four years. **The Battle of the Selle October 17th-25th**—followed by the **Battle of Maubeuge November 1st-11th** —sent the Germans in rapid retreat from the neighbourhood of Courtrai. This series of battles split the Germans into two parts, one on each side of the barrier of the Ardennes. The pursuit of the Germans was ended on November 11th, 1918, when the Armistice was signed.

Only in one remote corner of the world was the war carried on until November 25th—a German outpost in German East Africa. A bold commander had carried on guerilla warfare there during the whole of the war.

INDIAN MEMORIAL, Neuve Chapelle (*top*) see page 18.
[Photo: *The Times.*

CANADIAN MEMORIAL, Vimy Ridge, *see page 19.*

MEMORIALS TO THE MISSING AND NATIONAL MEMORIALS.

(Belgium and France).

THE ORDER FOLLOWED IS GEOGRAPHICAL— FROM THE SEA TOWARDS SWITZERLAND.

ZEEBRUGGE.

The Zeebrugge Memorial overlooks the sea ; the attack on the German submarine base in the Bruges canal was one of the most daring exploits of the Great War. This audacious deed was begun on the eve of St. George's Day, April 23rd, 1918, under the direction of Admiral of the Fleet, Sir Roger Keyes ; he had under his command the block-ships *Intrepid*, *Iphigenia* and *Thetis*, the cruiser *Vindictive* to attack the mole, two ferry boats, the *Daffodil* and *Iris* and the Submarine C3, besides monitors, destroyers, speed launches and motor boats ; in addition were the *Brilliant* and *Sirius* for Ostend Harbour. The attack on the mole was made by the *Vindictive*, *Daffodil* and *Iris* ; the Submarine C3 was blown up in order to destroy the viaduct and aid the landing parties on the mole ; the block ships were sunk in the channel of the canal and remained during the war an effective barrier to German submarines and destroyers.

This dramatic story has won a place in human history. The memorial has inscribed on it the words " In Memory of St. George's Day, 1918, when every moment had its deed and every deed its hero."

NIEUPORT.

The Nieuport Memorial, which is the first of the memorials to the Missing from the Channel side, is near the town of Nieuport and 16 kilometres S.W. of Ostend. Nieuport is on the river Yser, which enters the sea about two miles distant, and the Yser canal runs from Furnes to Bruges through the village ; these waters were important for the flooding operations which stopped the German advance between Nieuport and Dixmude. From 1914 till 1917, this section of the battle line was relatively quiet ; the Memorial records the names of those who fell in the operations during this period on the Belgian coast, and who lie in undiscovered graves ; the place in which the Memorial stands is within the British line ; it is a pylon with a bronze band on which are the names of 566 sailors, soldiers and marines ; the monument stands on a triangular platform ; a recumbent lion facing outwards is at each angle of the triangle.

CREST FARM, PASSCHENDAELE.

The Memorial Pillar at Crest Farm, Passchendaele, 12 kilometres N.E. of Ypres, is approached by stone flags ; this point was regarded as of great technical advantage and the Canadians encountered desperate resistance, but the farm was taken by the 4th Division, October 30th, 1917. The Memorial bears the inscription, " The Canadian Corps, in October-November, 1917, advanced across this valley—then a treacherous morass—captured and held the Passchendaele Ridge."

GRAVENSTAFEL.

This Memorial erected at Gravenstafel, 7 kilometres N.E. of Ypres, marks the capture by the New Zealanders of Gravenstafel on October 4th, 1917 ; it is similar in design to the Memorial at Longueval.

ST. JULIEN.

On April 22nd, 1915, a warm bright day, the 1st Canadian Division at St. Julien, 6 kilometres N.E. of Ypres resisted a terrible German onslaught ; they saw a heavy greenish-yellow cloud rolling from Langemarck ; it was the first time poison-gas was used in the War and against which there was no protection. The monument has been erected to commemorate the resistance of the Canadians and is one of the most striking in Belgium. From a grey tall column of stone there emerges as from a sheath the head and shoulders of a Canadian soldier, keeping watch over the 2,000 dead below ; the head, wearing a helmet bends forward ; the hands of the soldier are folded over a reversed rifle. There is nothing on the front save the word " Canada " ; an inscription on the sides reads : " This column marks the battlefield where 18,000 Canadians on the British left withstood the first German gas attacks the 22nd-24th April, 1915. Two thousand fell and here lie buried."

TYNE COT.

The Tyne Cot Memorial has been built between Passchendaele and Zonnebeke, 10 kilometres N.E. of Ypres ; it forms the North-Eastern Boundary of the largest British Cemetery on the Western Front ; here lie amid peaceful rural scenes the remains of nearly 12,000 British soldiers. There is probably no more impressive or beautiful cemetery in Belgium or France. This was the arena of the most desparate offensive fighting of the British forces in Belgium and the cross is set upon a German Blockhouse with the inscription : " This was the Tyne Cot Blockhouse, captured by the 2nd Australian Division, 4th October, 1917." The memorial proper, is a semi-circular wall broken by pillars, behind which are apses ; the wall and apses have carved in Portland Stone the names of 34,957 soldiers who fell from August 16th, 1917 to the end of the war and who have no known graves. The central apse contains the names of the men of the New Zealand Division, who fell at Broodseinde and the first battle of Passchendaele, October, 1917, and " whose graves are known only to God." The names on this memorial and on the Menin Gate, show better than any written words, how men from every part of the British Empire shared in this tragedy ; the introduction to the Registers of Ypres and Tyne Cot, published by the Imperial War Graves' Commission, refers to " the advance of the 2nd Worcesters at Gheluvelt, the resistance of the first Canadian Division before Poelcapelle, the desperate gallantry of the Australians and New Zealand troops at Polygon Wood and at Gravenstafel, the sacrifice of the South African Brigade at Messines, the Lahore Division standing in the gap at St. Julien."

The Ypres salient and the fierce attacks and stubborn resistance associated with its name, can never be forgotten ; the story has a place amongst the great battles of history and the Menin Gate and Tyne Cot will remain sacred places as long as our race endures.

BUTTES.

The Buttes Memorial (New Zealand), in Polygon Wood near Zonnebeke, 8 kilometres N.E. of Ypres, is built on a thickly wooded hill ; the memorial on the south west side of the Buttes New British Cemetery is to those officers and men of the New Zealand Expeditionary Force who fell in the Polygon Wood sector between September, 1917 and May, 1918, and whose graves, " are known only to God." The 348 missing soldiers belonged to the Otago, Wellington, Auckland and Canterbury regiments and other units. The road leading to the wood is nearly a mile north of the main road, between Menin and Ypres ; there are two cemeteries here, one called the Polygon Wood Cemetery, and the other the Buttes New British Cemetery ; the name Buttes refers to an artificial mound on which has been erected the Battle Memorial of the 5th Australian Division.

YPRES (Menin Gate).

The Ypres salient and the fierce attacks and dauntless resistance associated with its name, will shine for ever on the pages of British history. The Menin Gate is a monument of endurance that has probably never been surpassed in human history ; it is for the British people, one of the most hallowed spots in Europe and pilgrimages will be made to Ypres from home and from the uttermost ends of the earth by "generations yet unborn." An atmosphere of brooding sorrow hovers over this memorial with its stately severity and moving inscriptions. No one can read without emotion Simonides epigram, written over 2,000 years ago, "Stranger tell the Spartans that we lie here obeying their commands " ; the words on the Menin Gate, like the Greek epigram, are chaste and simple, " To the armies of the British Empire who stood here from 1914-1918 and to those of their dead who have no known graves." The word "stood" has in this setting a fullness of meaning and tragic content that is probably without parallel in the English language.

Ypres, like Troy was left with " her towers wrecked, her gods' houses things of dust, her altars waste." Ypres has imperishable records of doom, victory and defeat ; within the Gate the walls and alcoves are filled with scores of thousands of names of our people, who lie around the gate unburied, and every name represents defeat ; in presence of the lifeless dust of youth and faith and hope, we realise something of the hollowness of victory and the irreparable loss of the courage, heroism and idealism that speaks to us with winged words from these names carved in stone. They recall the immortal words of Euripides—

> " How are ye blind
> Ye treaders down of cities ; ye that cast
> Temples to desolation ; and lay waste
> Tombs ; the untrodden sanctuaries where lie
> The ancient dead, yourselves so soon to die."

On the Menin Gate are the names of 54,896 officers and men from the United Kingdom, Australia, Canada, Royal Newfoundland Regiment, New Zealand Expeditionary Force, South Africa, British West Indies and India.

HARLEBEKE.

This Newfoundland Memorial was erected at Harlebeke near Courtrai, 16 kilometres E. of Ypres to commemorate the advance of the Regiment at Ledeghem on October 14th, 1918. The Memorial erected on the bank of the river Lys, is a large bronze Caribou bugling his battle challenge from an artificial mound resembling a hill top.

HILL 62.

A Memorial Pillar has been erected on the summit of Hill 62 above Sanctuary Wood, 8 kilometres S.E. of Ypres ; it states, that "here at Mont Sorrel and on the line from Hooge to St. Eloi, the Canadians fought in the defence of Ypres, April-August, 1916." The approach is by a well-constructed road, which leads by a series of terraces to the summit ; all around are maples, holly, yew, heather and flowers. There is a very extensive view from the hill over this fiercely contested area ; Ypres, Poperinghe, the lake at Zillebeke, Hill 60, the Messines Ridge, the round summit of Mont Kemmel, St. Julien, Langemarck and Gheluvelt, are visible ; arrows on the coping indicate the situation of villages and towns stamped indelibly on the minds of the generation that lived through the War.

MESSINES RIDGE.

The Messines Ridge Memorial (New Zealand) to the missing, is within the British Cemetery and lies 10 kilometres S. of Ypres. It consists of a circular wall of rubble built around a mound on which the cross that is characteristic of cemeteries is erected. The encircling wall has panels of Portland stone let into it, on which are the names of 840 officers and men from New Zealand, "who fell in or near Messines in 1917 and 1918, and whose graves are known only to God."

ARRAS (*top*) see page 20.

CAMBRAI, see page 22.

MESSINES.

The Messines (New Zealand) Battle Exploit Memorial, is built on a hillock outside the village of Messines and 10 kilometres S. of Ypres ; it is a white stone obelisk with a terrace and garden encircling it. The Memorial commemorates "the action of the New Zealand Division, who captured the ridge on the 7th of June, 1917, and advanced 2,000 yards through Messines to their objective." Engraved on the Memorial are the words : " From the uttermost ends of the earth."

PLOEGSTEERT.

Ploegsteert Memorial is built on the Ypres side of the village of Ploegsteert and is 14 kilometres S. of Ypres ; on one side of the road is the Hyde Park Corner Royal Berks Cemetery and on the other the Berks Cemetery Extension, with the memorial to the missing ; the entrance is guarded by two recumbent lions and the building on which the names of 11,447 missing, are inscribed, is a circular colonnade enclosing an open space. It covers the period from October, 1914 till November, 1918 ; in this area, trench warfare lasted longest. The Memorial is to the officers and men who fell " between the river Douve and the towns of Estaires and Fournes." The names of the various battles are carved on the outside of the circular wall.

CITÉ BONJEAN.

The Cité Bonjean (New Zealand) Memorial is in the Military Cemetery of Cité Bonjean one kilometre W. of the town of Armentières ; the memorial proper is on the left and near the centre of the Cemetery boundary ; it is a semi-circular screen wall to which are fixed panels with the names of 48 officers and men from New Zealand, who fell in the neighbourhood of Armentières during 1916-17, and whose graves have not been discovered.

V.C. CORNER.

The Memorial is in the V.C. Corner, Australian Cemetery, 3 kilometres N.W. of Fromelles and about 10 kilometres S. of Armentières. The cemetery contains the graves of 410 Australian soldiers who were unidentified after the attack at Fromelles on July 19th and 20th, 1916. In this battle there fell also 889 officers, non-commissioned officers and men, who lie in undiscovered graves. A screen wall records the names of all the 1,299 Australian soldiers who fell and whose graves are not known. The battle in which so many Australian soldiers fell was the first serious engagement of the Australians in France.

NEUVE-CHAPELLE.

The Neuve-Chapelle Indian Memorial is 5 kilometres N. of La Bassée ; the place where it is erected was known during the war as Port Arthur ; the Memorial is Oriental in design and one of the most beautiful on the Western front ; in the foreground rises a tall column based on a podion on which rest two tigers ; the column which is about 50 feet high has a lotus leaf capital above which is a crown. From the podion on either side radiate pierced stone railings which embrace a half-circle terminating in two small buildings. The other half of the circle is a solid wall on which are inscribed the names of 4,847 soldiers of the Indian army who "fought in France and Belgium, 1914-1918 and in perpetual remembrance of those of their dead, whose names are here recorded and who have no known grave." In the column, both inside and outside the enclosure, are the words, "God is one, His is the victory." The names of those who fell in Belgium and are in unrecorded graves, are carved on the Menin Gate at Ypres , the Neuve-Chapelle Memorial in France serves also as a battle memorial of all the Indian units who were active in France and Belgium during the period of the War. The Memorial encloses a grass lawn at the centre of which is the " Stone of Remembrance."

LE TOURET.

The Le Touret Memorial in the cemetery of the same name, is 8 kilometres E. of Bethune Railway Station and about the same distance from the Indian Memorial at Neuve-Chapelle. Its position in a peaceful rural plain remote from city traffic, adds to its impressiveness ; an open rectangular court is enclosed by three walls ; on the fourth side is a colonnade. The names of 13,479 officers and men, who fell between October, 1914 and 25th September, 1915 and have no known graves, are inscribed on panels in arched recesses, and on the walls of the court ; around the open court are the names of seven battlefields where the missing lie. The stone for the Memorial was brought from Nimes in the South of France.

LOOS.

Loos Memorial, 6 kilometres N.W. of Lens Railway Station, is in Dud Corner Cemetery and records "the names of 20,693 officers and men of the army of the British Empire who fell after the 24th September, 1915 in the battles of Loos and Bethune and other activities in the neighbourhood of Loos and whose graves are not known." The Memorial forms the two sides and back of Dud Corner Cemetery ; " it stands almost on the site of a German strong point, the Lens Road Redoubt, captured by the 15th (Scottish) Division on the first day of the battle " ; on the walls are panels bearing the names of the missing and at the farther end are circular open courts and between the courts alcoves or apses, where the names are continued ; the five regiments most largely represented, are the King's Own Scottish Borderers, the Highland Light Infantry, the Black Watch, the Cameron Highlanders and the Gordon Highlanders.

VIMY RIDGE.

The Canadian Memorial at Vimy Ridge, 14 kilometres N. of Arras, is Canada's National Memorial in France, erected on Hill 145, opposite the King's Observation Post ; it is the highest point of Vimy. Canada took Vimy Ridge on the 12th April, 1917, and never afterwards lost it. This territory, which they won and retained, was conceded to them in perpetuity by the French Government. The Park itself and the dug-outs should be visited. The Memorial is built to commemorate Canada's achievements in the Great War and to preserve in stone the names of her soldiers who fell in France and whose graves are unknown ; carved on its walls are the names of 11,285 missing.
The Vimy Memorial is not yet completed, but enough has been done to warrant the view that, when unveiled, it will make a profound impression ; its situation overlooking the great coalfields, the view across the Douai plain, and southwards to the heights of Monchy-le-Preux, and its height which is about 125 feet, rivets the observer's attention ; it is no exaggeration to say of the Memorial itself, that in majesty of conception and grandeur of design, it is one of the most important pieces of work of modern times. In the foreground is a retaining wall with a tomb in front, over which broods the figure of Canada ; the apartness of this piece of sculpture and the attitude symbolising the tragic loneliness of grief is arrestive. Two groups, one on either side of the steps leading to the platform and enclosing walls, are singularly impressive, and the virile figures on the pylons, one of which bears the crown and maple leaves and the other the Fleur de Lys and the Laurel, symbolise the unity of purpose of France and Canada. The momument voices in stone great heroism, the defeat and victory of youth, and the constancy and fearlessness of this great western people. The stone that has been used in the construction of the Memorial, was found after prolonged investigation on the coast of Yugo-Slavia in Dalmatia.

ARRAS.

The Memorial at Arras in the Faubourg-d'Amiens Cemetery on the outskirts of the town is a cloister with a long colonnade and an apse, which contains the Memorial of the Flying Services, erected behind the Stone of Remembrance. This memorial is to commemorate the dead of the Royal Naval Air Service, the Royal Flying Corps and the Royal Air Force, who fell on the Western Front. In addition to the names on this Air Memorial, there are 34,924 on the cloister walls. The two sections of the Memorial have a total of 35,942 names of officers and men who have no known graves. The unfluted columns of the cloister are reminiscent of the Doric style. The undiscovered dead airmen were from Great Britain, Canada, Australia, New Zealand, South Africa and India.

MONCHY-LE-PREUX.

The Newfoundland Memorial at Monchy-le-Preux, 8 kilometres E. of Arras, commemorates the battle at Monchy-le-Preux on 14th April, 1917, in which the Regiment was engaged ; a bronze caribou has been erected on a devastated building in the village.

DURY.

The Memorial at Dury, 12 kilometres S.E. of Arras, commemorates the events during the second battle of Arras, 1918 ; on the Drocourt-Quéaunt line, the switch of the Hindenburg line was reputed to be impregnable ; the 1st and 4th Canadian Divisions broke through this line and took the village of Dury on September 2nd, 1918. The pillar bears the words : " the Canadian Corps, 100,000 strong attacked at Arras on August 26th, 1918, stormed successive German lines and here on September 2nd broke and turned the main German position on the Western Front and reached the Canal du Nord."

VIS-EN-ARTOIS.

Vis-en-Artois Memorial is at the back of the cemetery facing the road leading from Arras to Cambrai ; Vis-en-Artois is 12 kilometres S.E. of Arras ; the Memorial records the names of 9,868 officers and men from Great Britain and Ireland and South Africa, who fell in the final advance in 1918 in Artois and Picardy, and who have no known graves ; the names are recorded on panels on screened walls and two flanking carved walls ; the centre part of the screen wall has two enormous towering pylons, one marked 1914 and the other 1918. Behind the stone of remembrance on the screened wall, there is a noteworthy relief of St. George and the Dragon.

GUEUDECOURT.

This Newfoundland Memorial at Gueudecourt, 4 kilometres S. of Bapaume, has been erected chiefly to commemorate the success of the Newfoundland Regiment in capturing Rainbow Trench on October 12th, 1916 ; a bronze Caribou—the badge of the Regiment—stands on an artificial mound resembling a hillock.

LE QUESNOY.

The capture of Le Quesnoy, 25 kilometres N.E. of Cambrai, by the New Zealanders, is commemorated in this Memorial. The subject of the sculptured panel let into the wall is the scaling of the walls of the historic old fortress. To the right of the panel there is a winged figure symbolic of Victorious Peace.

THIEPVAL (*top*) *see page 23*.

NEWFOUNDLAND MEMORIAL, Beaumont Hamel, *see page 22*.

BOURLON WOOD.

The Memorial at Bourlon Wood 10 kilometres W. of Cambrai, is set in beautiful surroundings; the wood is about 350 feet high and dominates the neighbourhood; its capture was a very difficult feat. The inscription reads: " The Canadian Corps, on 27th September, 1918, forced the Canal du Nord and captured this hill. They took Cambrai, Denain, Valenciennes and Mons; then marched to the Rhine with the victorious allies."

CAMBRAI.

The Cambrai Memorial in the Louverval Military Cemetery, is situated to the left of the main road leading from Bapaume to Cambrai; the distance between these two towns is 29 kilometres, and the Memorial is almost midway between them. The history of Cambrai is checkered with battles since the days of Charlemagne and in the Great War it was occupied by the Germans until the beginning of October, 1918, although the British had advanced to within one mile of the city in November, 1917. During the operations between 20th November and 3rd December 1917, the losses were very heavy amongst which were 7,048 officers and men, who rest in unknown graves; it is to these that the memorial has been erected. Two pieces of sculpture are worthy of attention one of which represents a wounded soldier being borne on a stretcher, whose hand expresses great agony; the other vividly portrays five soldiers in a trench, one of whom having been shot, his revolver drops from a lifeless hand.

THE MASNIÈRES.

This Newfoundland Memorial was erected to commemorate the capture of Masnières on November 20th, 1917. Its chief feature is a bronze caribou—the badge of the Regiment. Masnières is 10 kilometres S. of Cambrai.

GRÉVILLERS.

Grévillers (New Zealand) Memorial in Grévillers British Cemetery, is near the village and 5 kilometres W. of Bapaume; this memorial relates to the Somme battles between March and August, 1918, and the final victorious advance from August to November, 1918.
The names of 455 officers and men from New Zealand are carved on panels fixed to a stone screen wall with an inscription relating the events commemorated, and the fact that " their graves are known only to God."

BEAUMONT-HAMEL.

Beaumont-Hamel Memorial Park, planted with trees from Newfoundland, is 84 acres in extent and situated 10 kilometres north of Albert; it commands an extensive view of the valley of the Ancre; the Memorial has been erected on ground over which the Newfoundland regiment fought at the beginning of the Somme Battle in July, 1916; the funds to purchase the park were supplied by the government and women of Newfoundland. The Memorial has two features, one of which centres in the figure of a huge Caribou standing on a mound of granite and clay, and the other in cast bronze panels which bear the names of 820 officers and men of the Royal Newfoundland Regiment, the Newfoundland Royal Naval Reserve and the Newfoundland Mercantile Marine, who fell in the War and whose graves are unknown. Shell holes, barbed wire, rusty helmets, broken guns, dugouts and trenches have been preserved, though the restorative hand of nature is effacing some of the grimer aspects of this deadly battlefield.

COURCELETTE.

At Courcelette a Memorial has been erected to commemorate the fighting of the Canadians in that battle zone; it is 11 kilometres N.E. of Albert; the Canadians arrived during the last week in August in the Somme district and fought in what is now known as the Flers-Courcelette battle. The monument is built on a hill, which is decorated with flowers; it bears the inscription: "The Canadian Corps bore a valiant part in forcing back the Germans on these slopes during the battles of the Somme, September 3rd-November 18th, 1916."

THIEPVAL.

The Thiepval Memorial is 8 kilometres N. of Albert. When one has seen the Menin Gate, the Thiepval Memorial compels comparison and we realise that they are complimentary; the Menin Gate is intimate and brings grief home to us. The massive Thiepval Memorial situated on a hill overlooking the valley of the Ancre with its terrible history of carnage, emphasises the loneliness and solitude of death; the builders sought out one of the "high places" of the district, which was called "the Red Zone" and the monument in lonely apartness speaks of the dead, whose dust is scattered far and wide over the Somme area. It is designed in the spirit of the 20th century; no ornate decoration detracts from its purpose. Straight lines predominate which are only broken by arches forming sixteen piers on which are inscribed the names of 73,367 British officers and men who fell between July, 1916 and March, 1918, "to whom the fortune of war denied the known and honoured burial given to their comrades in death." Stone wreaths embellished with oak leaves encircle the names of the battlefields where the unburied dead sleep; every name on the monument speaks of hopes blighted and youth overwhelmed by death, at the gateway of life; the Thiepval Memorial stands there "lest we forget."
The Memorial was unveiled by H.R.H. the Prince of Wales, K.G., on July, 31st, 1932.

POZIÈRES.

The Pozières Memorial is 6 kilometres N.E. of Albert on the Albert-Bapaume main road and encloses Pozières British Cemetery. The front is an open arcade terminating in small buildings. In the middle are the entrance buildings and gates; the sides and back are of stone and rubble and inserted in these are stone tablets which bear the names of 14,690 officers and men who fell in the Somme battlefields between 21st March and 7th August, 1918, and who lie in unknown graves. The Corps and Regiments most largely represented, are the Rifle Brigade, the Durham Light Infantry, the Machine Gun Corps, the Manchester Regiment and the Royal Horse and Royal Field Artillery.

DELVILLE WOOD.

The South African Memorial in Delville Wood, has been erected outside the village of Longueval and opposite the cemetery; it is 14 kilometres E. of Albert. The Memorial occupies a site in a wood 140 acres in extent; the approach to it is across a rectangular grass plot flanked by young oaks, which have been grown from acorns brought from Fransch Hoek in the Cape Province; the seeds or saplings from which these grew were taken by the Hugenots to South Africa after the revocation of the Edict of Nantes in 1685. There are relics of the fierce bombardment round Delville Wood in the burnt scarred tree trunks. The Memorial is not only to those soldiers from South Africa who fell on the Western Front, but to all from South Africa "who made the great sacrifice on the battlefields of Africa, Asia and Europe and on the sea." Above the Great Arch of the Memorial, which stands on the highest point of the ground are inscribed the words:
"Their ideal is our legacy
Their sacrifice our inspiration."

Through the arch northwards is seen the Cross of Consecration and southwards in the cemetery the Cross of Sacrifice. The arch is flanked on both sides by a semi-circular wall terminating in two covered buildings. Steps lead upward to the flat roof where there are arrows indicating the most important features of the neighbouring battlefields and the sites of memorials. The great arch has graven in panels the eight chief battle areas where the South Africans fought ; the stone dome crowning the Memorial supports a bronze group of two men leading a War Horse into battle. The old forest tracks are being kept open and have stone pillars bearing names which were given to them during the War, such as Regent Street, Bond Street, Rotten Row, Campbell Street.

LONGUEVAL.

The New Zealand battle exploit Memorial at Longueval, 16 kilometres N.E. of Albert, stands on the site of the Switch Trench and at the junction of the roads from Longueval to Flers and Courcelette ; it takes the form of a column standing on a projecting base in which are 4 panels ; on the front panel is an exquisite sculptured design of Maori carving, surrounding the words New Zealand and the fern-leaf.

CATERPILLAR VALLEY.

Caterpillar Valley (New Zealand) Memorial, in the Caterpillar Valley Cemetery is a quarter of a mile west of the village of Longueval and 12 kilometres E. of Albert. The Memorial records" the names of officers and men of New Zealand who fell in the Battles of the Somme, September and October, 1916, and whose graves are known only to God." There are eleven panels on screened walls, and on ten of these the 1,273 names are carved.

LE QUESNEL.

The Memorial at Le Quesnel, 26 kilometres S.E. of Amiens, commemorates the advance of the Canadians in 1918 ; the inscription reads : " the Canadian Corps, 100,000 strong on August 8th, 1918, attacked between Hourges and Villers—Bretonneux, and drove the enemy Eastward for eight miles." The advance was checked by unexpected reserves in the neighbourhood of Le Quesnel, but the following evening this and many other villages were taken.

SOISSONS.

Soissons is on the Aisne near the famous Chemin des Dames, built by Louis XV for the Royal Princesses ; the town is 102 kilometres from the Gare du Nord, Paris ; the town is very old and has been occupied frequently during the course of its history ; it has a famous cathedral, which is built on an elevated portion of ground above the river ; the towers of the cathedral have not been rebuilt since the War. The Memorial to the missing, near the left bank of the Aisne, has been erected between the cathedral and the river, which here is crossed by a bridge locally known as the Pont des Anglais. The Memorial records the names of 3,987 officers and men who lie in unknown graves and who fell between May and July, 1918 ; the following divisions are represented on the Memorial : the 8th, 15th (Scottish), 19th (Western), 21st, 25th, 34th, 50th (Northumbrian), 51st (Highland), 62nd (West Riding) ; the men from these divisions played a conspicuous part around Soissons in the critical months of 1918.

MARFAUX.

Marfaux (New Zealand) Memorial in the British Cemetery at Marfaux, is one kilometre from the village and 18 kilometres S.W. of Rheims. This Memorial takes the form of a panel in the record building near the Stone of Remembrance ; the panel contains the names of a sergeant and nine privates of the New Zealand Cyclist Battalion, who played a distinguished part in the capture of Marfaux ; the names are of those who fell in July, 1918 and whose graves are unknown.

LA FERTÉ-SOUS-JOUARRE.

La Ferté-sous-Jouarre is 66 kilometres from the Gare de l'Est, Paris ; the bridge which spans the swiftly flowing yellow Marne is about one kilometre from the station ; on the left bank of the river across the bridge on a triangular plot of land the monument has been erected ; it is built on a raised platform and four stone piers at the corners of the platform bear the coats of arms of England, Scotland, Wales and Ireland ; the Memorial proper, is a rectangular block of masonry surmounted by a sarcophagus, the names on stone panels are of the 3,888 officers and men who fought at Mons, Le Cateau and on the Marne and the Aisne during the early critical months of the War and who rest in unknown graves. The land between the monument and the river is planted with evergreens.

The bridge across the Marne had been blown up by the Germans and a floating bridge was constructed by the Royal Engineers of the 4th Division under fire ; two small monuments on circular plinths mark the ends of this temporary bridge.

NEW ZEALAND MEMORIAL, Messines, *see page 18.*

DIVISIONAL MEMORIALS.

British.	Situation.
GUARDS	GIVENCHY AND LES BOEUFS, 11 kilometres N.E. of Albert.
1st	LE CATEAU, (La Groise) 25 kilometres S.E. of Cambrai.
7th	MAMETZ, 8 kilometres E. of Albert.
7th	ZONNEBEKE, 10 kilometres N.E. of Ypres.
9th	PONT DE JOUR, 8 kilometres N.E. of Arras.
12th	MONCHY-LE-PREUX, 6 kilometres S.E. of Arras.
12th	EPEHY (Somme), 1 kilometre West of Epehy Railway Station.
14th	BELLEVARDE RIDGE, 4 kilometres E. of Ypres.
15th	BUZANCY, 8 kilometres S. of Soissons.
16th	GUILLEMONT, 12 kilometres E. of Albert.
16th	WYTSCHAETE, 8 kilometres S. of Ypres.
18th	THIEPVAL, 6 kilometres N. of Albert.
18th	TRONESWOOD, 9 kilometres E. of Albert.
18th	CLAPHAM JUNCTION, HOOGE, 8 kilometres E. of Ypres.
19th	LA BOISELLE, 5 kilometres N.E. of Albert.
19th	MONTAGNE DE BLIGNY, 15 kilometres S.W. of Reims.
19th	WYTSCHAETE, 8 kilometres S. of Ypres.
20th	LANGEMARCK, 6 kilometres N.E. of Ypres.
20th	GUILLEMONT, 9 kilometres E. of Albert.
25th	BAILLEUL,
29th	BEAUMONT HAMEL, 10 kilometres N. of Albert.
34th	LA BOISELLE, 10 kilometres N.E of Albert.
34th	MOUNT NOIR, 12 kilometres S.W. of Ypres.
34th	LANGEMARCK, 6 kilometres N. of Ypres.
36th	THIEPVAL, 6 kilometres N. of Albert.
37th	MONCHY-LE-PREUX, 10 kilometres E. of Arras.
41st	FLERS, 14 kilometres N.E. of Albert.
42nd	TRESCAULT, 14 kilometres E. of Bapaume and 13 kilometres S.W. of Cambrai.
46th	BELLENGLISE, 10 kilometres N. of St. Quentin.
46th	VERMELLES-HULLUCH Road, 8 kilometres S.E. of Bethune.
47th	HIGH WOOD, LONGUEVAL, 10 kilometres N.E. of Albert.
49th	ESSEX FARM Cemetery, 3 kilometres N. of Ypres.
50th	WIELTJE, 4 kilometres N.E. of Ypres.
51st	BEAUMONT HAMEL, 10 kilometers N. of Albert.
55th	GIVENCHY, 8 kilometres E. of Bethune.
56th	ARRAS.
58th	CHIPILLY, 11 kilometres S. of Albert.
62nd	HAVRINCOURT, 16 kilometres E. of Bapaume and 12 kilometres S.W. of Cambrai.
63rd	BEAUCOURT SUR ANCRE, 8 kilometres N. of Albert.
66th	LE CATEAU

Australian.	
1st	POZIERES, 6 kilometres N.E. of Albert.
2nd	MOUNT ST. QUENTIN, 5 kilometres N. of Peronne.
3rd	SAILLY-LE-SEC, 9 kilometres S.W. of Albert.
4th	BELLENGLISE, 11 kilometres N. of St. Quentin.
5th	POLYGON WOOD, 10 kilometres E. of Ypres.

Canadian.	
1st	THELUS, 12 kilometres N. of Arras.
3rd	GIVENCHY-EN-GOHELLE Road, 13 kilometres N. of Arras.

MEMORIALS TO REGIMENTS, BATTALIONS, BRIGADES, ETC.

Units.	Situation.
HOUSEHOLD CAVALRY	ZANDVOORDE 10 kilometres S.E. of Ypres.
1st KING EDWARD'S HORSE	VIEILLE CHAPEL COMMUNAL CEMETERY, 10 kilometres N. of Bethune
82nd FIELD COMPANY R.E.	BAZENTIN LE PETIT, 7 kilometres N.E. of Albert.
177th TUNNELLING COMPANY R.E.	RAILWAY WOOD, BELLEVARDE SPUR HOOGE, 5 kilometres E. of Ypres.
2nd BATTALION DEVONSHIRE REGIMENT	BOIS DE BUTTES, 23 kilometres N.W. of Reims.
7th YORKS REGIMENT	FRICOURT BRITISH CEMETERY, 6 kilometres E. of Albert.
ROYAL WELCH FUSILIERS	MAMETZ DANTZIG CEMETERY, 8 kilometres E. of Albert.
1st BATTALION SOUTH WALES BORDERERS	GHELUVELT, 8 kilometres E. of Ypres.
GLOUCESTERSHIRE REGIMENT ...	HOOGE, 6 kilometres E. of Ypres.
2nd WORCESTERSHIRE REGIMENT	INVERNESS COPSE, 7 kilometres E. of Ypres.
1st BLACK WATCH (Royal Highlanders)	HIGH WOOD, 10 kilometres E. of Albert.
1st LOYAL NORTH LANCASHIRE REGIMENT	CERNY, 5 kilometres N.E. of Soissons.
1/4 LOYAL NORTH LANCASHIRE REGIMENT	VILLERS-GUISLAIN, 20 kilometres S.W. of Cambrai.
KING'S ROYAL RIFLE CORPS	POZIÈRES, 6 kilometres N.E. of Albert.
KING'S ROYAL RIFLE CORPS ...	HOOGE, 6 kilometres E. of Ypres.
12th BATTALION MANCHESTER REGIMENT	CONTALMAISON COMMUNAL CEMETERY, 6 kilometres N.E. of Albert.
12th BATTALION YORK & LANCASTER (Sheffield City Battalion)	SERRE, 17 kilometres N. of Albert.
SEAFORTH HIGHLANDERS ...	FAMPOUX, 10 kilometres E. of Arras.
1st QUEEN'S OWN CAMERON HIGHLANDERS	HIGH WOOD, 10 kilometres E. of Albert.
8th BATTALION OF THE ARGYLL & SUTHERLAND HIGHLANDERS	BEAUMONT HAMEL, 10 kilometres N. of Albert.
2nd BATTALION MUNSTER FUSILIERS ...	ETREUX BRITISH CEMETERY, 16 kilometres S.E. of Le Cateau.
TANK CORPS	POZIERES, 8 kilometres N.E. of Albert.
MONMOUTH REGIMENT	WIELTJE, 5 kilometres N.E. of Ypres.
2nd LONDON REGIMENT (47th Division)	FLERS, 14 kilometres N.E. of Albert.
QUEEN VICTORIA RIFLES	HILL 60, which is 8 kilometres S.E. of Ypres.
1st BATTALION LONDON SCOTTISH REGIMENT	MESSINES, 10 kilometres S. of Ypres.
64th INFANTRY BRIGADE	COJEUL BRITISH CEMETERY, 12 kilometres S.E. of Arras.
102nd & 103rd INFANTRY BRIGADES (Tyneside Scottish and Tyneside Irish)	LA BOISELLE, 5 kilometres N.E. of Albert.
MISSING OF MUNSTER	A Celtic Cross outside the Cathedral of YPRES.
1st AUSTRALIAN TUNNELLING COMPANY R.E.	HILL 60, which is 8 kilometres S.E. of Ypres.
CANADIAN CORPS ARTILLERY ...	THELUS, 11 kilometres N. of Arras.
85th BATTALION CANADIAN EXPEDITIONARY FORCE (Nova Scotia)	PASSCHENDAELE, 12 kilometres N.E. of Ypres.

SOUTH AFRICAN MEMORIAL, Delville Wood (*top*) see page 23

AUSTRALIAN MEMORIAL, Mount St. Quentin.

MEMORIALS ERECTED UNDER DIRECTION OF THE IMPERIAL WAR GRAVES COMMISSION IN ADDITION TO THOSE MENTIONED ON PAGES 14-25.

MEMORIALS IN EUROPE.

Belgium.

ZEEBRUGGE (Churchyard)	To the memory of three British officers and one mechanic who fell on the Mole at Zeebrugge, and have no known graves.

England.

BOURNEMOUTH	Memorial to certain officers and men lost locally and unburied.
CHATHAM	Memorial to British officers and men of the Imperial Navies who have no known grave but the sea.
DOVER	Memorial to certain officers and men lost locally and unburied.
HULL (Western)	Memorial to certain officers and men lost locally and unburied.
TOWER HILL, London	Memorial to officers and men of the Merchant Navy and the Fishing Fleet who lost their lives in the War and whose graves are in the sea.
PLYMOUTH	Memorial to officers and men of the Imperial Navies who have no known grave but the sea.
PORTSMOUTH ...	Memorial to officers and men of the Imperial Navies who have no known grave but the sea.
SOUTHAMPTON (Hollybrook Cemetery)	Memorial to 1,853 officers and men who were lost at sea and whose bodies were never recovered.
SOUTHEND	Memorial to certain officers and men lost locally and unburied.
WALTON-ON-THAMES	Memorial to certain officers and men lost locally and unburied.

France.

LE HAVRE	(1) To those whose bodies were not recovered when the hospital ship "Galeka" was sunk on 28th October, 1916.
	(2) To those whose bodies were not recovered when the "Normandy" was torpedoed on 25th January, 1918.
	(3) Records the death of 62 British soldiers, 3 unknown men and 22 men of the Egyptian Labour Corps whose bodies were not recovered after the loss of the hospital ship "Salta" on the 10th April, 1917.
NOYELLES-SUR-MER, near Etaples	Memorial to Chinese missing in France.

Germany.

COLOGNE (Southern Cemetery)	To the memory of twenty-five British officers and men who died in Germany and have no known graves.

Gibraltar.

NORTH FRONT CEMETERY.	To the men of the R.A.S.C. who were lost on the 3rd November, 1915, when the s.s. "Woodfield" was sunk.

Greece.

DOIRAN	To the British soldiers who fell in Macedonia and have no known graves.
MIKRA	To the nurses and soldiers from the United Kingdom, New Zealand and India, lost at sea from hospital ships and transports to and from Salonika.

Holland.	
THE HAGUE	To two naval ratings whose graves are unknown.
Italy.	
GIAVERA	To British officers and men who fell in Italy and have no known graves.
SAVONA ...	To those who perished in the s.s. "Transylvania."
Poland.	
POSEN (Old Garrison Cemetery).	To five armoured car ratings whose graves are not known.
N. Russia.	
ARCHANGEL	To British soldiers who fell in Northern Russia, and whose graves are unknown.
Turkey (Gallipoli).	
CHUNUK BAIR	To New Zealanders who fell in the Battle of Sari Bair and other battles, and have no known graves.
HELLES	To the missing from the United Kingdom and India, on land and sea, and certain Australian missing, whose graves are undiscovered.
HILL 60	To the New Zealanders who fell on Hill 60, August, 1915, and have no known graves.
LONE PINE	To the Australian and certain New Zealand soldiers who fell in the Gallipoli campaign, and have no known graves.
TWELVE TREE COPSE	To the New Zealanders who fell in the 2nd Battle of Krithia and have no known graves.
Turkey.	
HAIDAR PASHA (Istanbul).	To the British soldiers who died in Southern Russia, Georgia and Azerbaijan, and whose graves are unknown.

MEMORIALS IN ASIA.

Arabia.	
ADEN	To soldiers and sailors of the United Kingdom, New Zealand and India, who fell at Bab-el-Mandeb and have no known graves.
China.	
TSINGTAO	In British Military Cemetery, to British and Indian soldiers killed in the capture of Tsingtao, whose graves are unknown.
HONGKONG	To the Chinese of the Merchant Navy and other services whose graves are unknown.
HONGKONG (Mount Caroline Cemetery).	Memorial erected to one British soldier who perished in fire.
India.	
BOMBAY	(1) To Indian soldiers of the Royal Navy, the Royal Indian Marine and the Merchant Navy who fell in the Great War and whose graves are in the sea. (2) To officers and warrant officers of the Royal Indian Marine whose graves are unknown. (This Memorial is in St. Thomas's Cathedral.)
DELHI	To British and Indian soldiers who fell on or beyond the North-West Frontier, 1914-1921.
SHILLONG (in the Khasi and Jaintia Hills).	To men of the Assam Rifles and the Assam Military Police killed while maintaining order in Assam and Burma.

Iraq.
BASRA — To the soldiers of the forces of the British Empire who fell in the Mesopotamian campaigns or died as prisoners of war in Syria and Asia Minor, from 1914 to the end of August, 1921, and have no known graves.

Palestine.
JERUSALEM — To the soldiers of the British Empire (except the New Zealand soldiers who fell in Egypt and the Indian soldiers) who fell in Egypt and Palestine and have no known graves.

Persia.
RESHIRE (Suburb of Bushire).
(1) To British soldiers who fought and fell in and beyond Persia, and whose graves are unknown.
(2) To Indian soldiers who died in Persia and whose graves are unknown.

Siberia.
VLADIVOSTOCK — To the British soldiers who died in Siberia after the Treaty of Brest Litovsk.

MEMORIALS IN AFRICA.

East Africa.
DAR ES SALAAM (Capital of Tanganyika)
(1) To East African native troops and carriers.
(2) To British and Indian officers and men who died after January, 1917, and whose graves are not known.

MOMBASA
(1) To East African native troops and porters.
(2) To officers and men who died and were buried at sea off the coast of East Africa.

NAIROBI
(1) To East African native troops and carriers.
(2) To the British and Indian officers and men who fell in East Africa before the advance to the Rufiji in January, 1917, and who have no known graves.

TANGA (35 miles S. of border of Kenya). — To the British and Indian soldiers who fell in November 1914 at the attack on Tanga.

TANGA (Jasin). — To Indian officers and men who fell in 1915 at and near Jasin, 28 miles from Tanga.

Egypt.
CHATBY — To 982 soldiers of the United Kingdom, Australia and S. Africa who were mined or drowned in Egyptian waters and have no known graves but the sea.

GIZA — To men of the Egyptian Labour Corps and the Camel Transport Corps whose graves are unknown.

KANTARA — To the soldiers of New Zealand who fell in Egypt and have no known graves.

PORT TEWFIK (Suez). — To native soldiers of the Indian Army who fell in Egypt and Palestine.

The Gambia.
BATHURST — In MacCarthy Square, Bathurst, to the dead of the Gambia Infantry Company who are not commemorated elsewhere.

Nigeria.
ZARIA
LOKOJA ...
CALABAR — To the dead of the Nigeria Regiment.
IBADAN
KUMASI — To the missing of the Gold Coast Regiment.
ACCRA

Seychelles Islands.
MONT-FLEURI, Victoria — To the Seychelles Carrier Corps whose graves are unknown.

Somaliland.
BERBERA — To the officers and men who fell in Somaliland from 1914-1920. The panel is fixed to the west wall of the Shaab.

Italian Somaliland.
BARDERA FORT — To one Indian medical officer whose grave is not known

N. Rhodesia.
ABERCORN — To the Native Carriers, whose names and graves are not known.
IKAWA — To two men of the N. Rhodesian Rifles whose graves are unknown.
LIVINGSTONE — Memorial at the Headquarters of the N. Rhodesia Police to native soldiers who died between September 1914 and January 1919.

S. Rhodesia.
SALISBURY — To the British South Africa Police and the Rhodesia Native Regiment who fell during the war.

Sierra Leone.
FREETOWN — Erected in front of New Government Offices at Freetown to the men of the Sierra Leone units whose graves are unmarked.

West Africa.
LAGOS — To the Nigerian Marine, British ranks and ratings and African ratings, erected in the Colonial Church.
LAGOS — General memorial to the soldiers, sailors and carriers of Nigeria, and particularly the Carrier Corps and the Inland Water Transport.

MEMORIALS IN AMERICA.

Nova Scotia.
HALIFAX —
(1) Fort Massey Cemetery. To two men killed in the Halifax explosion.
(2) Overlooking Halifax Harbour. To Canadian soldiers, sailors, nurses and merchant seamen buried or lost at sea or killed in the Halifax explosion.

British Columbia.
VICTORIA — Memorial in Ross Bay Cemetery to Canadian naval ranks and ratings lost or buried at sea, 1917-1918.

MEMORIALS IN NEW ZEALAND.

New Zealand.
AUCKLAND ... ... — To men of the District who died at sea.
(Waikumete Cemetery)
CANTERBURY ... ... — To men of the District who died at sea.
(Bromley Cemetery).
OTAGO ... — To men of the District who died at sea.
WELLINGTON ... — To men of the District who died at sea.
(Karori Cemetery).

INCLUSIVE WEEK-END TOUR TO
YPRES, ARRAS AND THE SOMME
WITH OPTIONAL EXTENSIONS TO PARIS OR WIMEREUX.
Leaving LONDON every Saturday from May 20th to September 16th inclusive.

This tour covers practically the whole length of the old British front and visits in detail the Ypres Salient, Arras, Vimy Ridge and the Somme Sector. The tour from Boulogne is by motor with English speaking chauffeur who acts as guide. The charges indicated below are subject to a minimum of four persons travelling on each departure ; on dates when this minimum is not reached arrangements can be made for smaller numbers at a supplementary cost ; details can be obtained on application at any of our Offices.

ITINERARY.

Saturday. Leave LONDON (Victoria) at 9.00 a.m. for Folkestone and Boulogne which is reached at 12.25 p.m. Luncheon is provided on arrival. The motor tour commences at 2.0 p.m., the drive being via St. Omer, Cassel and Poperinghe to YPRES ; here the night is spent.

Sunday. The motor tour is continued after breakfast, the drive being through the Ypres Salient including Shrapne Corner, Zillebeke, Hill 60, Hellfire Corner, Menin Road, Sanctuary Wood, Hooge, Clapham Junction, Inverness Copse, Tyne Cot, Passchendaele, Poelcapelle, St. Julien, returning to YPRES in time for luncheon. In the afternoon the drive is via the Messines Ridge, Ploegsteert, Armentieres, Neuve Chapelle, La Bassee, Hill 70, Lôos, Lens, Vimy Ridge, Grange Tunnel, Souchez, Notre-Dame-de-Lorette to ARRAS. Dine and sleep at hotel.

Monday. The last section of the motor tour is commenced after breakfast, the route being via Bapaume, Flers, Longueval, Delville Wood, Caterpillar Valley, Bazentin, Pozieres, Thiepval, Newfoundland Memorial Park to ALBERT where luncheon is taken. After luncheon the drive continues via Doullens, Frevent, Hesdin, Montreuil to BOULOGNE which is reached in time to connect with the homeward boat leaving at 7.10 p.m. FOLKESTONE is reached at 8.40 p.m. and LONDON (Victoria) at 10.50 p.m.

OPTIONAL EXTENSION TO PARIS.

Saturday & Sunday. As above.

Monday. Clients proceed with the motor tour as far as ALBERT, leaving after luncheon by rail for Paris which is reached in time for dinner.

Tuesday to Friday. At PARIS, full accommodation being provided at the hotel each day. A whole day motor drive ROUND PARIS is arranged, visiting the principal places of interest.

Saturday. To LONDON. Accommodation terminates with breakfast after which clients proceed by rail to Boulogne and steamer to Folkestone, reaching LONDON (Victoria) at 3.30 p.m.

OPTIONAL EXTENSION TO WIMEREUX.

Saturday, Sunday and Monday as above. On reaching BOULOGNE on Monday afternoon clients are conveyed by motor to a good class hotel in WIMEREUX, accommodation commencing with dinner.

Tuesday to Friday. In WIMEREUX, the popular French seaside resort. Full accommodation is provided at the hotel each day.

Saturday. To LONDON. Accommodation terminates with breakfast, after which clients return via Boulogne and Folkestone to LONDON (Victoria) arriving at 3.30 p.m.

NOTE.—The period of stay in Paris or Wimereux can be amended to meet individual requirements; charges on application.

INCLUSIVE CHARGES FROM LONDON. TOUR No. BT. 1001.

MAIN TOUR.	WITH PARIS EXTENSION.	WITH WIMEREUX EXTENSION.
£8 8 0	£13 17 6	£11 2 6

The charges provide :—

1.—Return travel ticket from London 2nd class on steamers and 3rd class in England (in connection with the Paris Extension 2nd class travel is provided on the French railways).

2.—Seat in motor for the three-day battlefield tour as indicated including entrance fees and services of guide. (A whole day motor tour round Paris is included in the charge for the Paris extension).

3.—Full accommodation at good class hotels throughout the tour, consisting of room and three meals each day, commencing with luncheon on Saturday and terminating with luncheon on Monday, including gratuities to hotel servants and local taxes.

4.—Reserved seats on trains in England, and services of our local representatives.

" BRITISH MEMORIALS OF THE GREAT WAR, 1914-1918."
Most Comprehensive and Interesting.

Just Published.   —   **Price 1/-.**

Obtainable at any Office of Dean & Dawson, Limited.

INCLUSIVE EIGHT-DAY TOUR TO
OSTEND, YPRES, ARRAS & AMIENS

WITH OPTIONAL RETURN VIA PARIS.

Leaving **LONDON** every Saturday from **May 6th to September 30th** inclusive.

(With escort on the outward journey).

ITINERARY—TOUR No. BT. 1002.

Saturday. Leave LONDON (Victoria) by morning service for Dover and OSTEND, accompanied by our representative. Ostend is reached about 4.0 p.m., dinner and room being provided.

Sunday & Monday. At OSTEND. One day is devoted to a motor tour through the Battlefields to YPRES. A number of the places of special interest visited on this tour are shewn in the itinerary for Tour No. BT. 1004 on page 5.

Tuesday. To AMIENS. Leave Ostend after breakfast by rail for ARRAS, which is reached about 2.30 p.m. (Packed luncheon is provided for the journey.) A private motor car is waiting to meet clients on arrival at Arras for a sightseeing drive through the surrounding districts, including the 1916 front line, Vimy Ridge, and a number of British and French Cemeteries. The journey is continued, on termination of the drive, by rail to AMIENS where the night is spent. Dinner on arrival.

Wednesday. At AMIENS. The day is spent in an extensive tour by motor of the Somme Battlefield Area, including Thiepval. Luncheon at Albert ; dine and sleep at Amiens.

Thursday. To OSTEND. Leaving Amiens after breakfast proceed by rail to OSTEND. (Packed luncheon on route.) Dinner and room in Ostend.

Friday. At OSTEND—at leisure.

Saturday. To LONDON. Return after breakfast by steamer to Dover and rail to London which is reached about 4.30 p.m.

WITH PARIS EXTENSION TOUR No. BT. 1003.

Saturday to Wednesday.—As above.

Thursday. Leave Amiens after breakfast by rail for PARIS, which is reached about noon. Luncheon, dinner and room at hotel.

Friday. At PARIS—at leisure. All meals at the hotel.

Saturday. Leave Paris (St. Lazare) at 10.36 a.m. for Dieppe, Newhaven and LONDON, which is reached at 6.40 p.m.

NOTE.—The period of stay in Paris can be amended to meet individual requirements. Prices on application.

INCLUSIVE CHARGES FROM LONDON.

	Tour No.	" C " Hotels.	" B " Hotels.	" A " Hotels.
Main Tour	BT. 1002	£11 17 6	£12 15 0	£14 14 0
With Paris Extension	BT. 1003	£13 10 0	£14 7 6	£15 15 0

HIGH SEASON.—The charges are increased by 12/6 for departures taking place during the month of August. Additional charge for 1st Class travel on steamers : Tour No. BT. 1002, 11/- ; Tour No. BT.1003, 13/2.

The charges provide :
1. Travel tickets for the tour from London, second class on steamers and on the Continent, and third class in England.
2. Full accommodation at hotels in accordance with the grade selected, consisting each day of Continental breakfast, luncheon, dinner, room, light, and service, including gratuities to servants and all taxes.
3. Drives by motor car visiting the Battlefields in the surrounding districts of Ypres, Arras and Amiens as specified.
4. Transfers including hand baggage between stations and hotels and vice versa.
5. Services of escort on the outward journey from London to Ostend and of our local Representative in the centres visited.

SPRING & SUMMER HOLIDAYS.—Do not complete your arrangements until you have seen our programmes of inclusive holidays at home and abroad, by land, sea and air. These books are obtainable gratis at any of our offices.

THE BATTLEFIELDS IN ONE DAY

SPECIAL INCLUSIVE TOURS

Leaving **LONDON** every Monday, Thursday and Saturday from June 17th to September 16th inclusive.

(With escort on Saturdays).

YPRES AND THE MENIN GATE MEMORIAL

— No Passports Required. —

ITINERARY—TOUR No. BT. 1004.

Leave LONDON (Liverpool Street) at 8.30 p.m. by rail for Harwich, there embarking on L.N.E.R. steamer sailing at 10.10 p.m. for ZEEBRUGGE. (Sleeping berths are reserved.) Zeebrugge is reached at 5.30 a.m., passengers proceeding thence by electric tramway along the coast to OSTEND, the journey occupying about 70 minutes. English breakfast is provided in Ostend, after which the motor tour of the Battlefields is commenced.

The Ypres tour is perhaps the most impressive in the World. It traverses the Battlefields of Belgium and passes through towns and villages where literally "not one stone was left on another." Nieuport, Dixmude (with its trench of death), Essex Farm, Salvation Corner, Shrapnel Corner, Hill 60, Hell Fire Corner, St. Julien (the site of the Canadian Memorial), Houthulst Forest, Leugenboom (where the huge sixteen-inch gun known as Long Max was left behind undamaged during the final retreat of the Germans), are a few of the scenes visited. The main objective, however, is Ypres and here ample time is allowed for an inspection of the Menin Gate Memorial, the Cathedral, Cloth Hall, etc. Hot luncheon is provided in Ypres. On the return to Ostend about 7.0 p.m., dinner is provided, after which there is time for a look round Ostend before proceeding to Zeebrugge to join the homeward steamer sailing at 11.35 p.m. Arrive Harwich about 6.0 a.m. and LONDON (Liverpool Street) at 8.0 a.m.

YPRES, ARRAS, AND THE SOMME

(Passports Required)

ITINERARY—TOUR No. BT. 1005.

Leave LONDON (Liverpool Street) at 8.30 p.m. for Harwich, there embarking on L.N.E.R. steamer for ZEEBRUGGE. Clients are met on arrival at Zeebrugge at 5.30 a.m., where English breakfast is provided, the journey being continued thence by motor to YPRES. After an inspection of the Menin Gate Memorial the drive continues via Messines Ridge, Hyde Park Corner, over the French frontier, Armentieres, Neuve Chapelle, La Bassee, Loos, Lens, Vimy Ridge to ARRAS, where luncheon is provided. Time is allowed for an inspection of the town of Arras and the Memorial to the Missing at the Faubourg d'Amiens Cemetery. (See below for details of Somme extension.)

The return drive to ZEEBRUGGE is made via Lille and Bruges. Dinner is provided at Zeebrugge, after which clients embark on the homeward steamer sailing at 11.35 p.m. LONDON is reached at 8.0 a.m.

SOMME BATTLEFIELDS EXTENSION.—Clients booking for the Somme extension leave Arras after luncheon, the drive being via Bapaume, Albert, Beaumont-Hamel, Newfoundland Park (visit British trenches) and THIEPVAL, where an inspection is made of the Memorial to the Missing. Returning to Arras via Pozieres the main party is joined for the homeward drive to Zeebrugge.

INCLUSIVE CHARGES FROM LONDON.

Tour No. BT. 1004.	**52/6**	Tour No. BT. 1005.	**59/-**	With Somme Extension	**69/6**

These charges are for Monday and Thursday departures only. For Saturday departures there is a supplementary charge of 9/-.

Ask at our offices for details of reduced rate tickets to LONDON and HARWICH.

The charges provide:

1. Return travel ticket London, 2nd class on steamers and 3rd class in England.
2. Seat in motor for the Battlefields tour as indicated, including entrance fees and services of guide.
3. English breakfast, luncheon and dinner, including gratuities to waiters.
4. Reserved seats on trains, also berths on steamers (if available at the time of booking.) Clients travelling on Saturdays have the services of escort from London to Zeebrugge.

NOTE.—The extra charge for 1st class travel on steamers, if arranged at the time of booking, is 10/- return.

We are in a position to arrange for wreaths to be laid in the British War Cemeteries in France and Belgium, also for the taking of photographs of graves and cemeteries. Particulars can be obtained at any of our offices.

INCLUSIVE BATTLEFIELD TOURS—WITHOUT PASSPORTS
SPECIALLY ORGANISED FOR THE PURPOSE OF VISITING
WAR GRAVES

A facility of special interest to relatives wishing to visit War Cemeteries.

Many of the War Cemeteries in Belgium and France are in isolated situations some considerable distance from habitations and railways. In order to reach such cemeteries it is necessary for the journey to be made from the most convenient railway station by private car, and even when satisfactory transport is available, the cost is in many cases prohibitive. Realising this may mean the cancellation of a long desire to visit the grave of a relative, we have organised a series of one day " AREA " tours by motor, thus making such visits possible for those who have hitherto had to abandon the idea on the score of expense. Seven Areas have been selected, two departures of tours to each area being operated during the summer months. Clients participating in one of these tours will be able to visit any Cemetery they desire in the area in which they are interested, without additional charge. Ample time will be allowed for the taking of photographs, etc. Naturally the itineraries of the drives are somewhat elastic, being dependent upon the cemeteries to be visited on each particular tour. It is not possible in the space available for us to detail the names of the numerous cemeteries which are embraced in each area. Enquiries as to the area in which any Cemetery is situated will receive prompt attention. An important feature of these arrangements is that PASSPORTS ARE NOT NECESSARY. Details of the seven areas incorporated in this scheme together with particulars of the departure dates and inclusive charges from London are announced below. Departures can be arranged on other dates to meet the requirements of private party organisers. For all further information apply to the nearest Office of DEAN & DAWSON, LTD.

AREA TOURS Nos. 1 & 2. YPRES DISTRICTS A. and B.

District A. Departures July 8th and August 5th.
District B. Departures July 15th and August 12th.

ITINERARY.—Leave LONDON (Victoria) at 11.0 p.m., travelling via Dover, and reaching OSTEND at 5.0 a.m. the next day. Breakfast is provided at Ostend after which the motor tour is commenced. Hot luncheon is provided at Ypres and the tours include a visit to the Menin Gate Memorial. Ostend is reached on the return journey at 7.0 p.m. After dinner there is time for a look round Ostend before leaving at midnight for Dover and London, which is reached at 7.40 a.m.

INCLUSIVE CHARGES FROM LONDON.—Tour " A," 55 - ; Tour " B," 57/6.

AREA TOUR No. 3. ARMENTIERES, MERVILLE & NEUVE CHAPELLE

Departures June 19th and August 1st.

ITINERARY.—Leave LONDON (Liverpool Street) at 7.42 p.m., via Harwich. reaching ZEEBRUGGE about 6 a.m. the next day. Breakfast is provided at Zeebrugge, after which the motor tour is commenced. Hot luncheon is taken at Armentieres. Zeebrugge is reached on the return journey in time for dinner which is provided before the homeward journey is commenced at 11.35 p.m. London is reached at 8.0 a.m. the next day.

INCLUSIVE CHARGE FROM LONDON—63/-.

AREA TOURS Nos. 4/5. ARRAS DISTRICTS A. and B.

District A. Departures July 8th and August 5th.
District B. Departures July 22nd and August 19th.

ITINERARY.—Leave LONDON (Victoria) at 11.0 p.m. for Folkestone continuing thence by steamer to Dunkerque and rail to Arras, which is reached about 9.15 a.m. Breakfast is provided on arrival, after which the motor tour is commenced. Hot luncheon is provided en route, Arras being reached on the return in time for dinner. The homeward journey is commenced about 10.0 p.m. London being reached at 7.40 a.m. the next day.

INCLUSIVE CHARGE FROM LONDON—Tour " A " or " B," £4 17 6.

AREA TOURS Nos. 6/7. AMIENS DISTRICTS A. and B.

District A. Departures on July 15th and August 12th.
District B. Departures on July 29th and August 26th.

ITINERARY.—The journey from London to Amiens is via Folkestone/Dunkerque the same as for Tours 4/5, Amiens being reached at 10.8 a.m. Breakfast is provided on arrival, and hot luncheon during the motor tour. Dinner is taken in Amiens before the homeward journey is commenced about 9.0 p.m. London s reached at 7.40 a.m. the next day.

INCLUSIVE CHARGE FROM LONDON—Tour " A " or " B," £5 2 6.

The charges provide :—
1. Return travel ticket from London, third class throughout.
2. Seat in motor for the Battlefield tour, including the services of English-speaking guide.
3. English breakfast, luncheon, and dinner, including gratuities to waiters.
4. Reserved seats on trains, and services of our local representatives.

NOTE.—In connection with Tour 3, berths are reserved on the steamer between Harwich and Zeebrugge and vice versa without extra cost. Berths on the steamers between Folkestone and Dunkerque and vice versa in connection with Tours 4/5/6/7 can be reserved upon payment of a supplementary charge of 3/- in each direction.

A Deposit of 10/- secures a place in, and forms part of the charge for any of the Tours announced in this leaflet

DEAN & DAWSON LTD.

ESTABLISHED 1871. TRAVEL ORGANISERS AND SHIPPING AGENTS

ADMINISTRATION—7, BLANDFORD SQUARE, LONDON, N.W.1

Telegraphic Address—"Viaggio, Baker, London." Telephone No.—Paddington 8050-5 (6 lines)

TICKET AND ENQUIRY OFFICES

GREAT BRITAIN

ABERDEEN. 35a, Union Street (Mackay Bros. & Co.(Aberdeen) Ltd.)	'Phone 825.
BARNSLEY. 37, Eldon Street.	'Phone 219.
BATH. 7, New Bond Street (Bell & Co.).	'Phone 3705.
BIRMINGHAM, 2. 3, Ethel Street, New Street.	'Phone Midland 5206.
BOLTON. 2, Bradshawgate.	'Phone 320.
BOURNEMOUTH. 113a, Old Christchurch Road.	'Phone 351.
BRADFORD. 83, Market Street.	'Phone 2971.
BRIGHTON. 89, King's Road.	'Phone 3466.
CAMBRIDGE. 6, King's Parade (Bell & Co.)	' Phone 173.
CARDIFF. Borough Chambers, Wharton Street.	' Phone 5008.
CHESTERFIELD. 25, Cavendish Street.	'Phone 2619.
DONCASTER. 57, High Street.	'Phone 432.
DUNDEE. 9, Whitehall Crescent (Mackay Bros. & Co. (Dundee) Ltd.)	'Phone 5490.
EDINBURGH. 31-33, Hanover Street (Mackay Bros.)	'Phone 20151-2.
HALIFAX. 22, Horton Street.	'Phone 2919.
HARROGATE. 16, James Street.	'Phone 4155.
HUDDERSFIELD. 7, St. Peter's Street.	'Phone 571.
HULL. 7, King Edward Street.	'Phone 35663.
KIRKCALDY. 204, High Street (Mays, Ltd.).	'Phone 2200.
LEEDS. 51, Boar Lane.	'Phone 24859.
LEICESTER. 1, Gallowtree Gate.	'Phone 21683.
LINCOLN. 321, High Street.	'Phone 459.
LIVERPOOL. 6-10, Parker Street.	'Phone Royal 685.
LONDON. 81, Piccadilly, W.1.	'Phone Grosvenor 2873-6.
26, Aldersgate Street, E.C.1.	'Phone National 3716.
87, Gracechurch Street, E.C.3.	'Phone Monument 4432-3.
Imperial Hotel, Russell Square, W.C.1.	'Phone Terminus 5057.
MANCHESTER, I. 53, Piccadilly.	'Phone 6393-4 Central.
18, Piccadilly Corner Chambers, Gore Street.	
NEWCASTLE-ON-TYNE. Central Station.	'Phone 21862.
NOTTINGHAM. 3, Upper Parliament Street.	'Phone 44129.
OLDHAM. 2, Mumps.	'Phone Main 1513.
OXFORD. 137, High Street (Bell's Tvl. Ser.)	'Phone 2506.
PORTSMOUTH. 6, Pearl Buildings.	'Phone 6540.
ROCHDALE. Station Buildings, Maclure Road.	'Phone 3278.
ROTHERHAM. 32, Westgate.	'Phone 201.
SHEFFIELD. 42, Fargate.	'Phone 22288.
SOUTHAMPTON. Bank Chambers, Canute Road.	'Phone 2476.
STOCKPORT. 52, St. Petersgate.	'Phone 2597.

FRANCE

MARSEILLES. 10, Rue Beauvau.	Tel. Add. "Voyages."
MENTONE. (Seasonal) Square Bennett.	Tel. Add. "Voyages Menton."
NICE. 28, Rue Meyerbeer.	Tel. Add. "Travel."
PARIS. 2-4, Rue Edouard VII.	Tel. Add. "Raildeadar."

CONDITIONS OF BOOKING.

A booking deposit of 10/- each person secures a place in, and forms part of the charge for the tour. Balance of the charge is payable a week before departure.

Dean & Dawson Ltd. reserve to themselves the right to alter, amend or cancel any of the arrangements announced in their programmes should circumstances render this necessary, or to abandon a tour, and in the event of such abandonment by them of any tour, any money paid will be refunded in full, and the liability of Dean & Dawson Ltd. will then entirely cease.

The charges for tours announced in Dean & Dawson Ltd. programmes are calculated on the rates of exchange prevailing at the time of going to press, and are subject to revision in accordance with any fluctuations which may take place subsequently.

Dean & Dawson Ltd. do not accept any liability for damage, loss, injury or delay which may be incurred by a passenger holding tickets issued in connection with these arrangements, however occasioned, nor for any loss or damage to his or her property. Travellers are strongly urged to insure their baggage. Proposal forms can be obtained and policies can be issued on demand at any office of Dean & Dawson Ltd.

The issue of Through Tickets is subject to the conditions and regulations referred to in the time tables, books, bills and notices of the companies and proprietors on whose railways, steamers, coaches or air services they are available, and the companies or proprietors are not to be liable for any loss, damage, injury, delay or detention caused, or arising off their respective railways, steamers, coaches or air services. The contract and liability of the companies and proprietors are limited to their own railways, steamers, coaches and air services.

MAP NO 1 (YPRES)

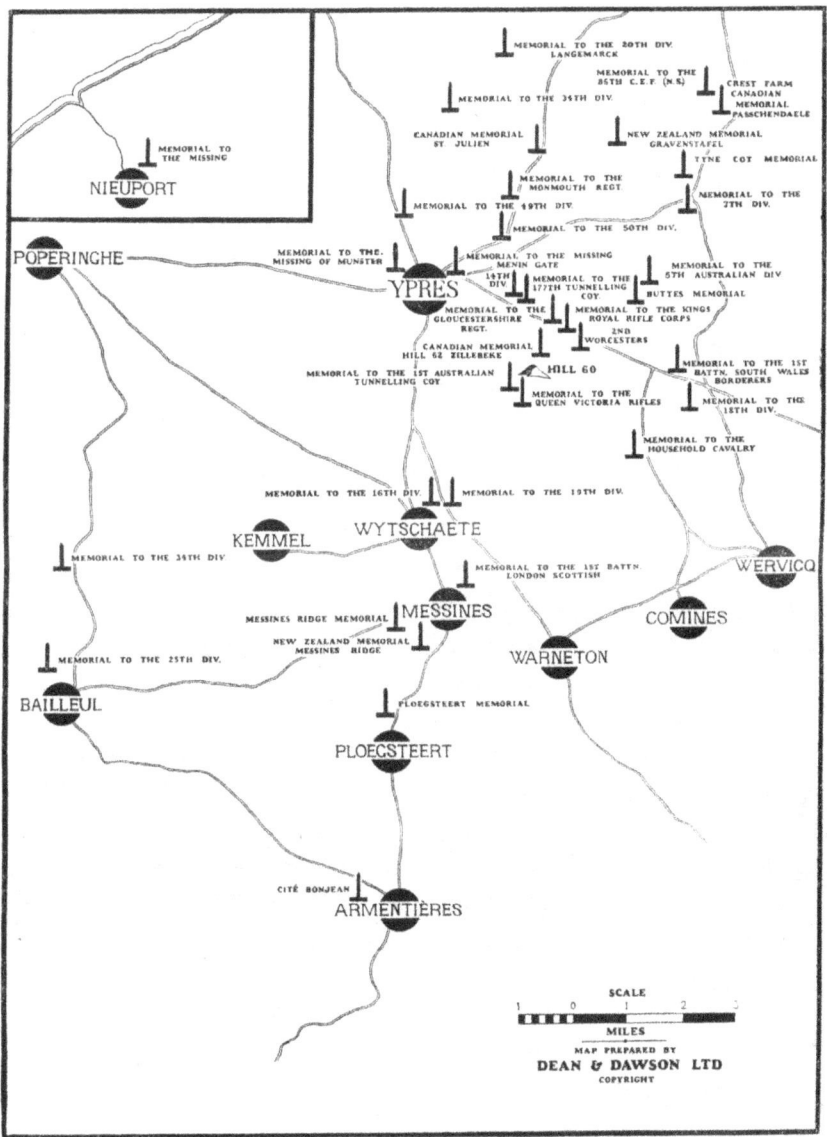

MAP NO. 2 (ARRAS)

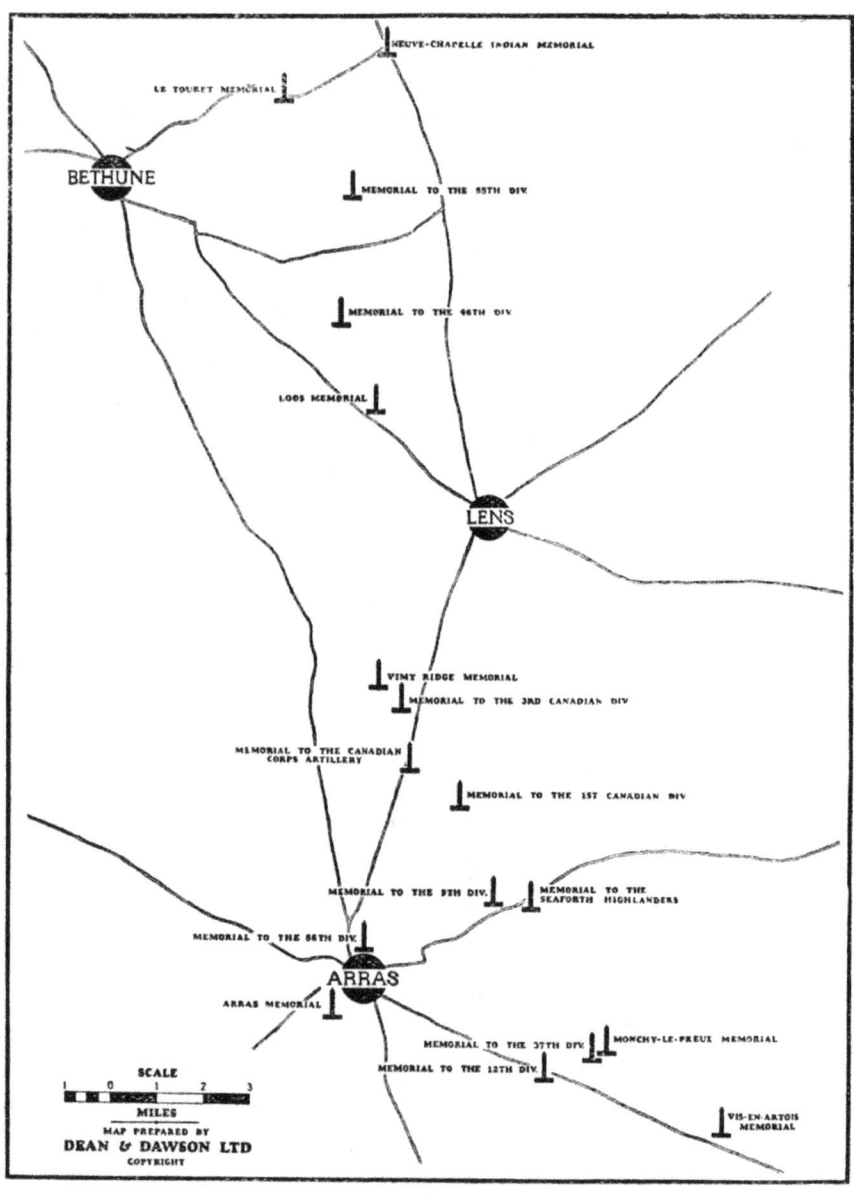

MAP NO. 3 (SOMME)

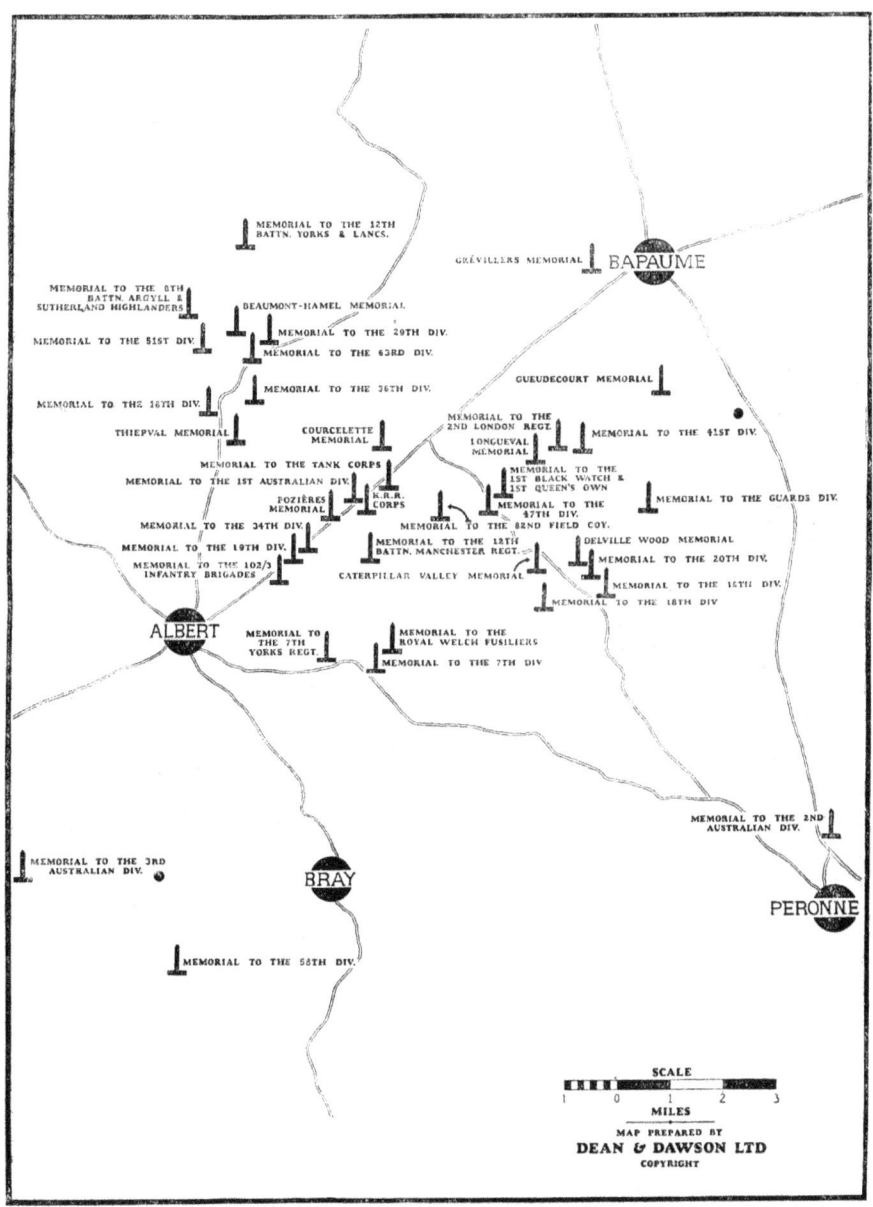

These Maps are issued by Dean & Dawson Ltd.
with their book entitled
BRITISH MEMORIALS OF THE GREAT WAR 1914-18 (Price 1/-).

MAP NO. 4 (CAMBRAI)

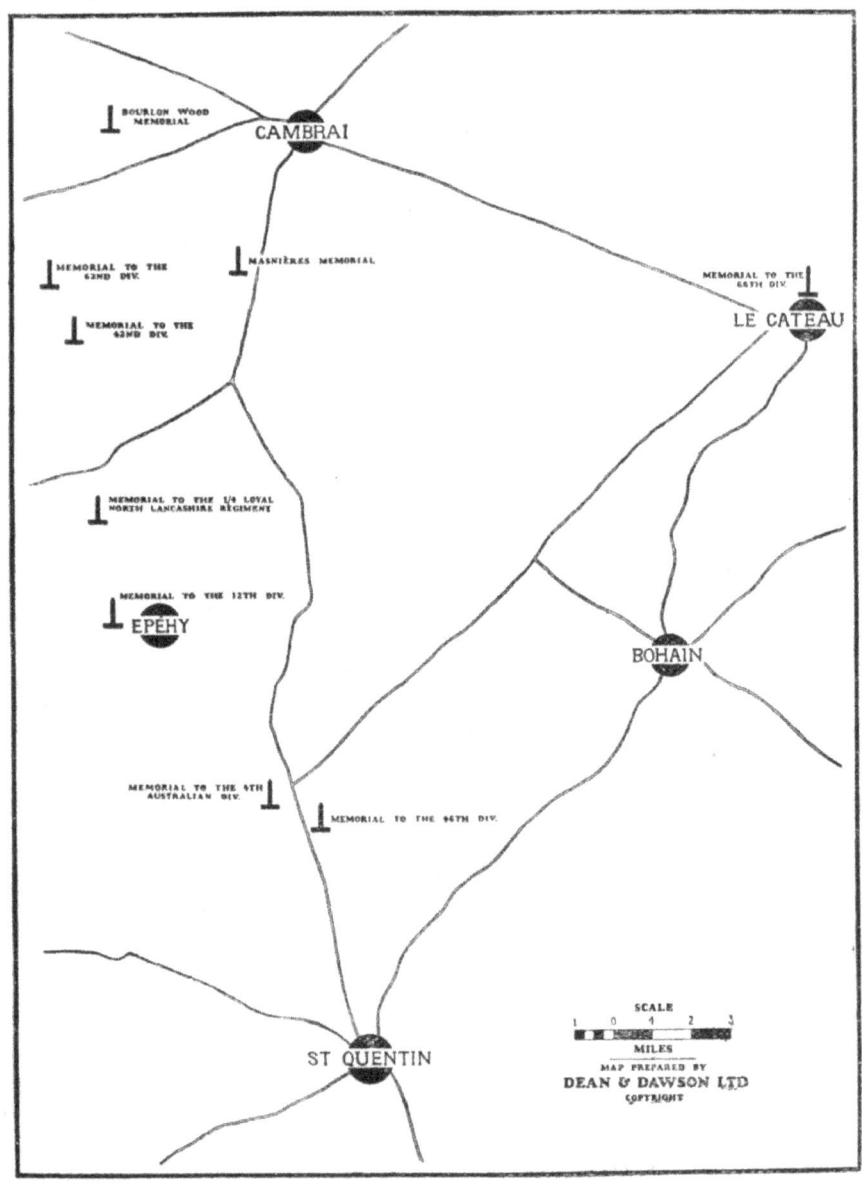

DEAN & DAWSON LTD.

ESTABLISHED 1871   TRAVEL ORGANISERS AND SHIPPING AGENTS

ADMINISTRATION—7, BLANDFORD SQUARE, LONDON, N.W.1

Tel. Add.—"Viaggio, Baker, London."   Telephone No.—Paddington 8050-5 (6 lines)

TICKET AND ENQUIRY OFFICES
GREAT BRITAIN

BARNSLEY. 37, Eldon Street. 'Phone 219.
BIRMINGHAM, 2. 3, Ethel Street, New Street. 'Phone Midland 5206.
BOLTON. 2, Bradshawgate. 'Phone 320.
BOURNEMOUTH. 113a, Old Christchurch Rd. 'Phone 351.
BRADFORD. 83, Market Street. 'Phone 2971.
BRIGHTON. 89, King's Road. 'Phone 3466.
CARDIFF. Borough Chambers, Wharton Street. 'Phone 5008.
CHESTERFIELD. 25, Cavendish Street. 'Phone 2619.
DONCASTER. 57, High Street. 'Phone 432.
HALIFAX. 22, Horton Street. 'Phone 2919.
HARROGATE. 16, James Street. 'Phone 4155.
HUDDERSFIELD. 7, St. Peter's Street. 'Phone 571.
HULL. 7, King Edward Street. 'Phone 35663.
LEEDS. 51, Boar Lane. 'Phone 24859.
LEICESTER. 1, Gallowtree Gate. 'Phone 21683.
LINCOLN. 321, High Street. 'Phone 459.
LIVERPOOL, 1. 6-10, Parker Street. 'Phone Royal 685.
LONDON. 81, Piccadilly, W.1. 'Phone Grosvenor 2873-6.
26, Aldersgate Street, E.C.1. 'Phone National 3716.
87, Gracechurch Street, E.C.3. 'Phone Monument 4432-3.
Imperial Hotel, Russell Square, W.C.1. 'Phone Terminus 5057.
MANCHESTER, 1. 53, Piccadilly. 'Phone 6393-4 Central.
18, Piccadilly Corner Chambers, Gore Street.
NEWCASTLE-ON-TYNE, 1. Central Station. 'Phone 21862
NOTTINGHAM. 3, Upper Parliament Street. 'Phone 44129.
OLDHAM. 2, Mumps. 'Phone Main 1513.
PORTSMOUTH, 6, Pearl Buildings. 'Phone 6540.
ROCHDALE. Station Buildings, Maclure Road. 'Phone 3278.
ROTHERHAM. 32, Westgate. 'Phone 201.
SHEFFIELD. 42, Fargate. 'Phone 22288.
SOUTHAMPTON. Bank Chambers, Canute Rd. 'Phone 2476.
STOCKPORT. 52, St. Petersgate. 'Phone 2597.

FRANCE

MARSEILLES. 10, Rue Beauvau. Tel. Add. "Voyages."
MENTONE. (Seasonal) Square Bennett. Tel. Add. "Voyages."
NICE. 28, Rue Meyerbeer. Tel. Add. "Travel."
PARIS. 12, Boulevard de la Madeleine. Tel. Add. "Raildeadar."

ITALY
ROME. Piazza Colonna (under management of C.I.T.). Tel. Add. "Italotours."

NORTH AFRICA.
ALGIERS. 37, Rue d'Isly (Hignard Freres).
CAIRO. 4, Nubar Pasha Street (David Jamal & Son). Tel. Add. "Jamco."
TUNIS. 65, Avenue Jules Ferry (Hignard Freres) Tel. Add. "Burville."

NORTH AMERICA
NEW YORK. Frank Tourist Co., 542, Fifth Avenue. Cable Add. Franktour, New York. 'Phone Vanderbilt 9126.

SEASONAL OFFICES

BELGIUM & HOLLAND
Blankenberghe, Bruges, Brussels, Flushing, Ostende.

GERMANY
Berlin.

SWITZERLAND
Grindelwald, Lucerne, Lugano, Wolfenschiessen.

VISITS to the BATTLEFIELDS

or a particular grave or cemetery are arranged most satisfactorily through

DEAN & DAWSON LTD.

who also undertake to lay wreaths as desired and in addition are authorised to photograph graves.

www.ingramcontent.com/pod-product-compliance
Lightning Source LLC
Chambersburg PA
CBHW041322110426
42743CB00052B/3481